SHARING HEART

SHARING HEART

KAREN HOOD DELRASO

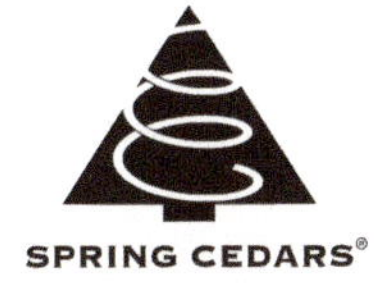

First edition, 2023

Photography by Karen Hood DelRaso
Book design by Spring Cedars

ISBN 978-1-950484-72-0 (paperback)
ISBN 978-1-950484-69-0 (hardback)

Published by Spring Cedars
Denver, Colorado
www.springcedars.com

This book is dedicated to my mother Loretta Hood,
who always had unwavering faith in love
and inspired me throughout my life.

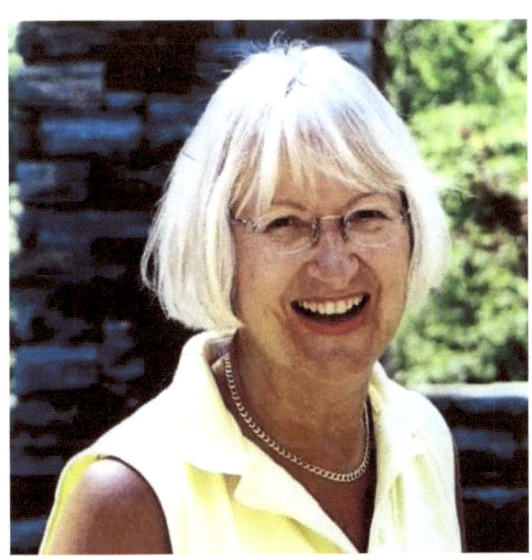

This is a gift from me to you. May your heart always be open to the love and beauty that surround you!

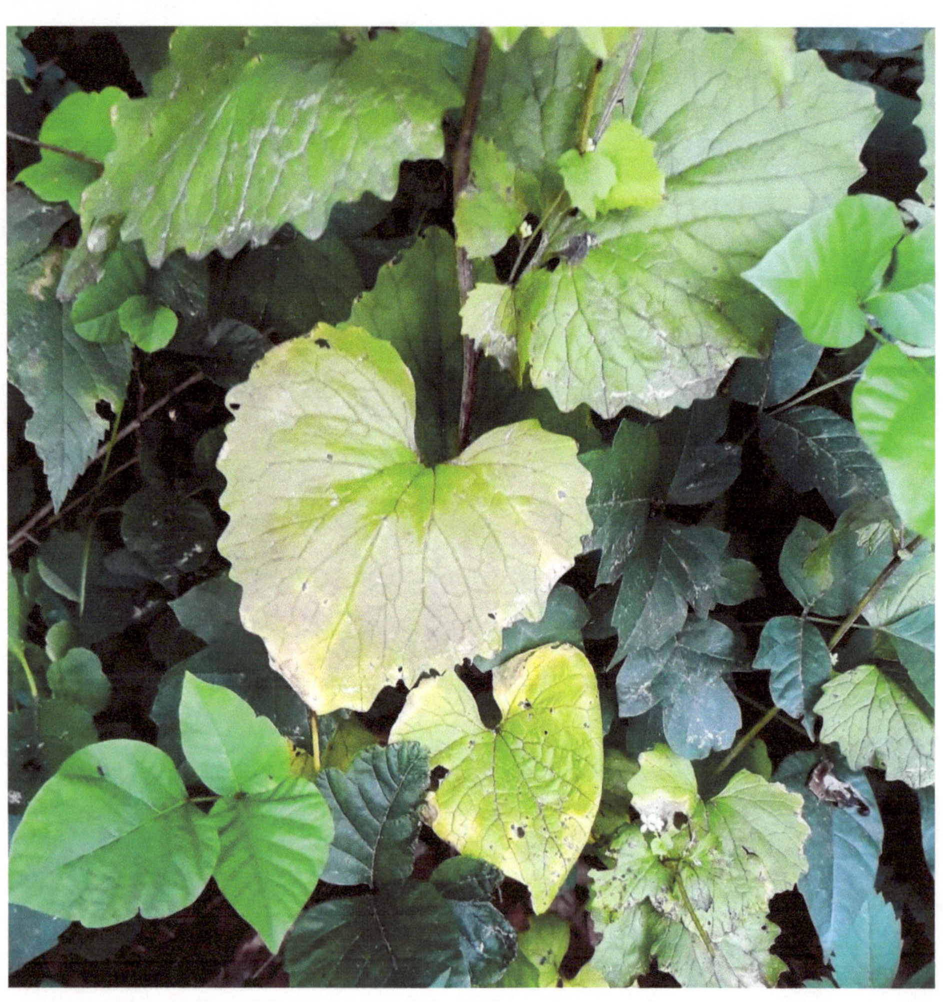

After my mother's passing, I was feeling lost. I wondered if everything would be okay. One day, while out chasing rainbows, I encountered a glorious sight in the sky.

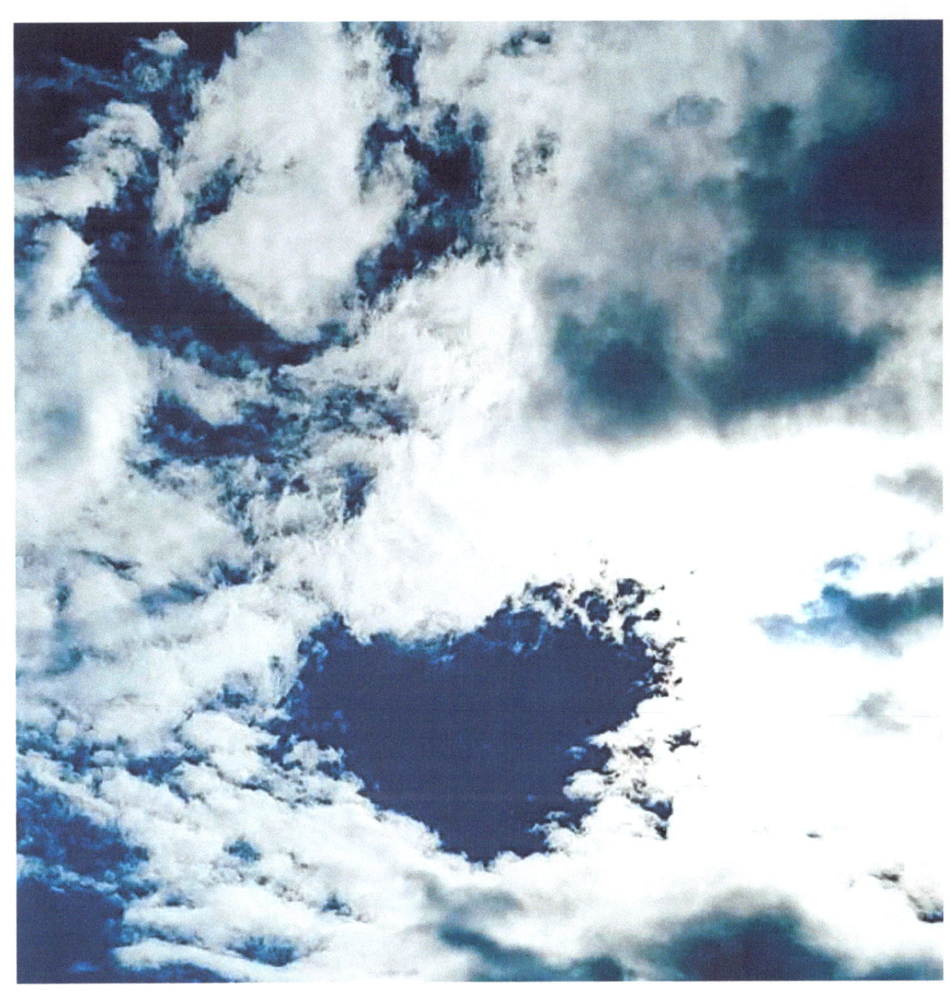

From that moment, my eyes were opened to seeing the love and beauty of nature around us, and that everything would be okay.

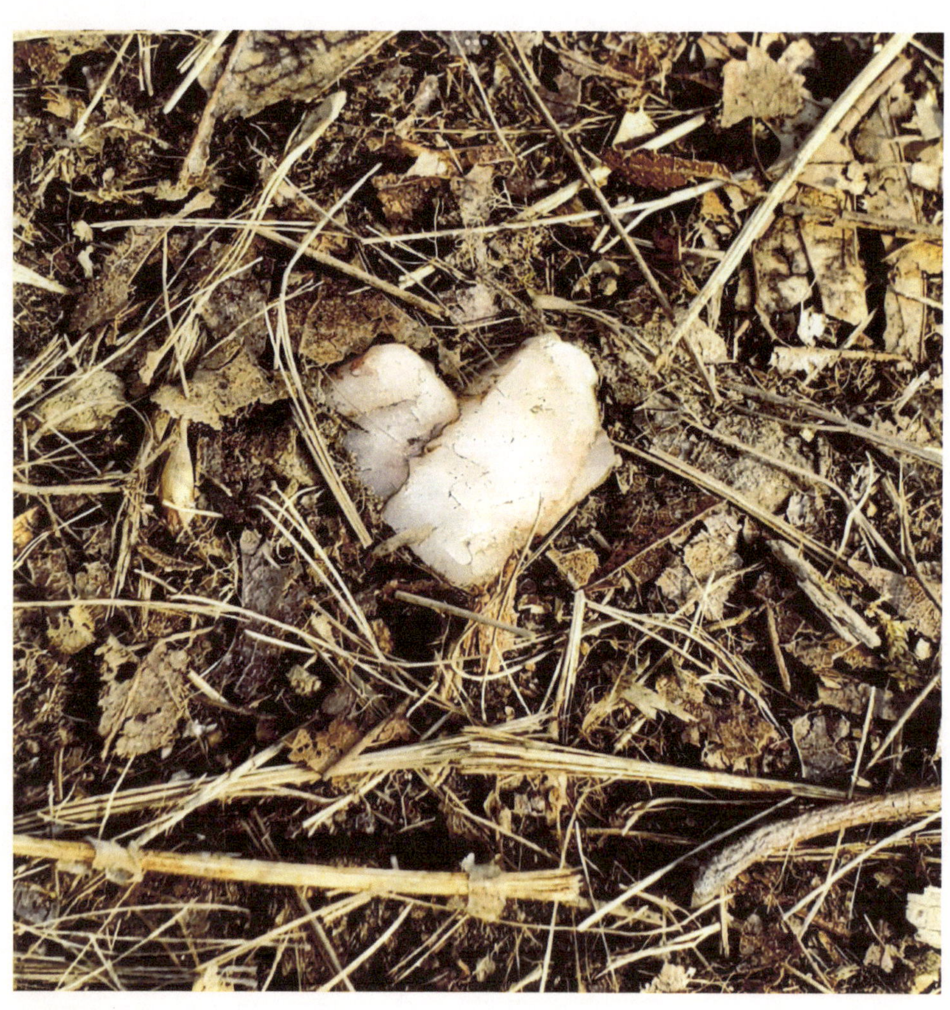

Discovering hearts in nature and sharing them with others helped me reconnect with people.

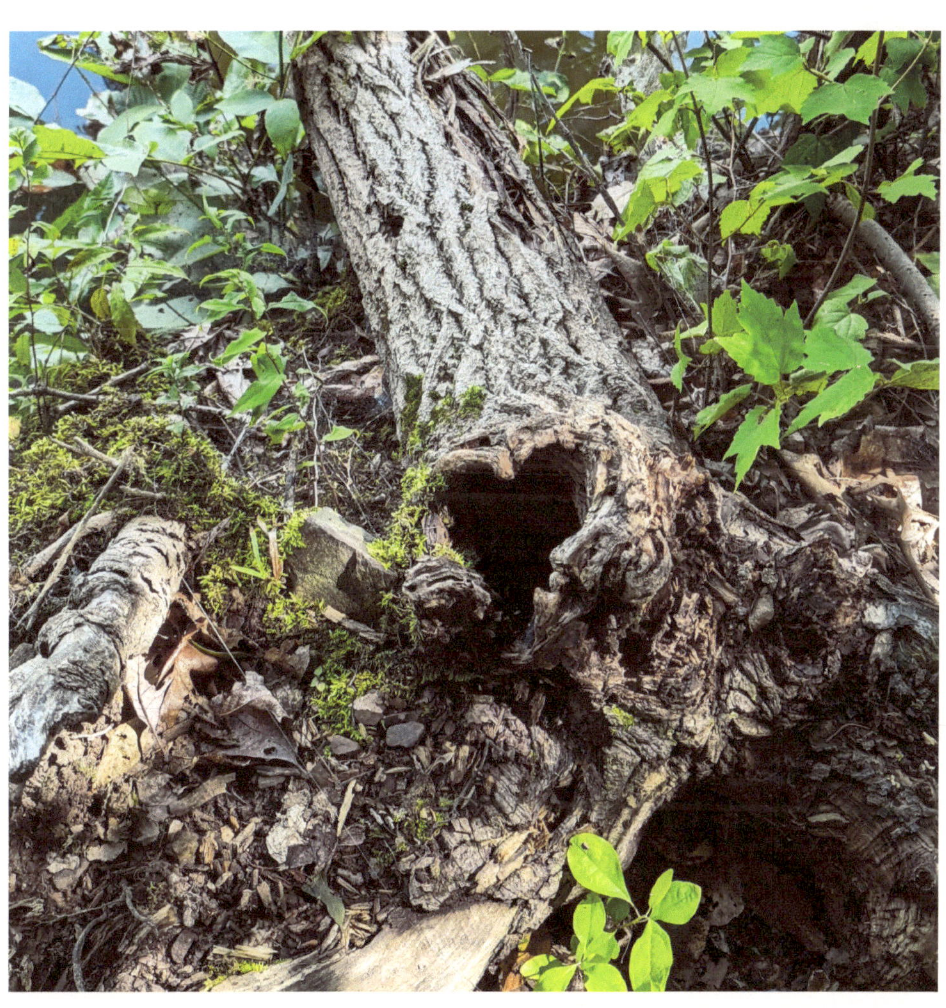

Every time I saw a heart, it made me smile, whether I was out for a walk or having a hard day. I started noticing how the simple sight of one could improve my mood.

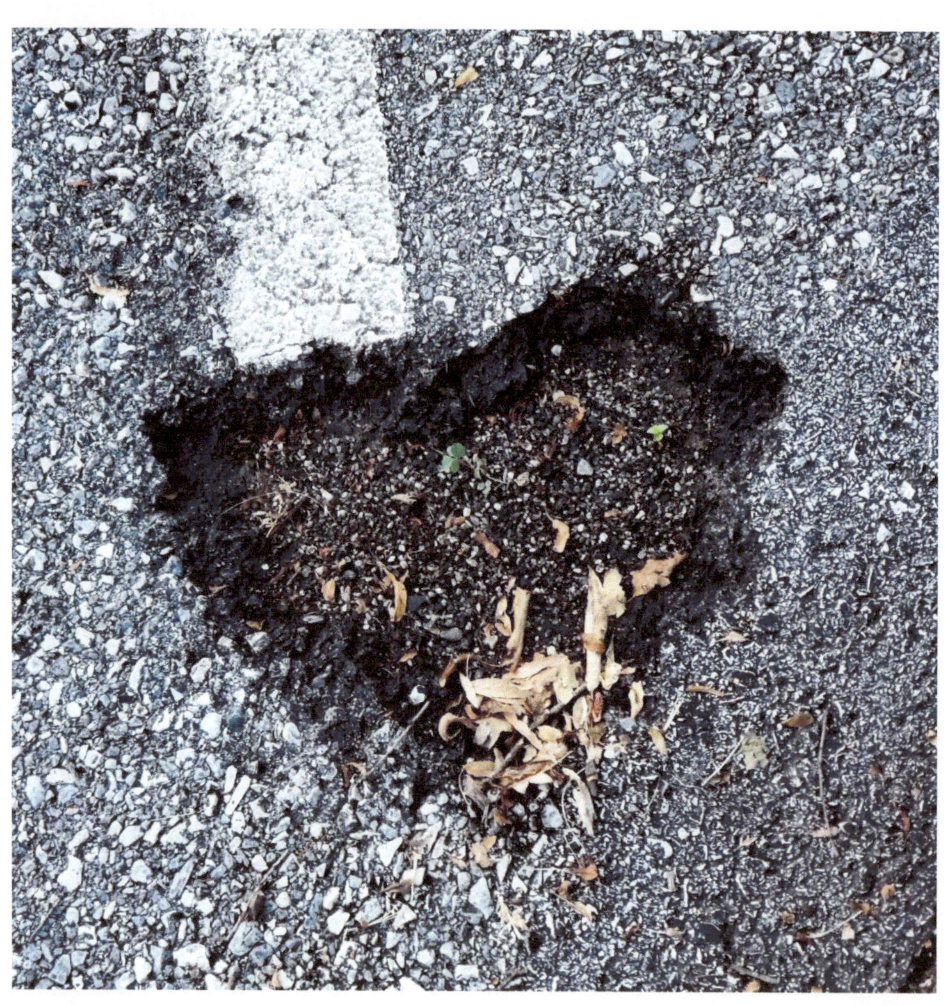

This is when I began sharing these hearts with family, friends, and strangers. With some who were struggling, and others who were searching for joy.

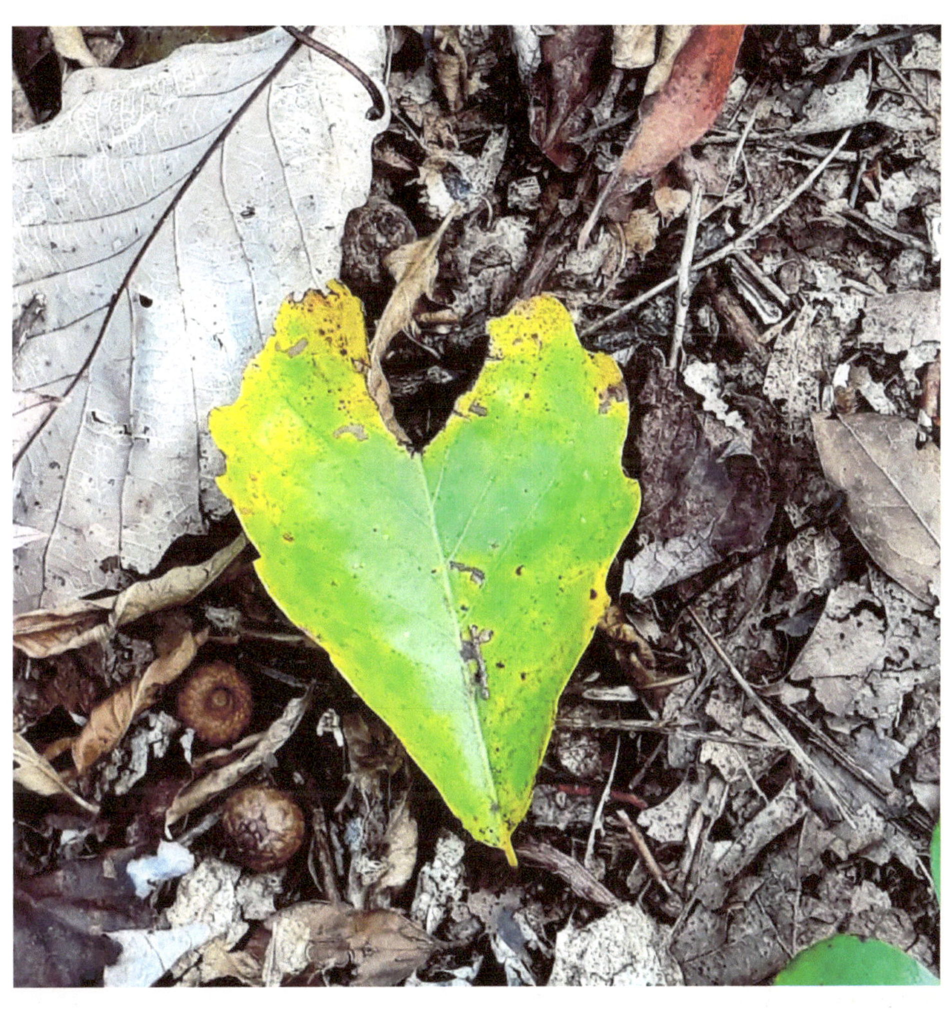

My hope was that it would help them as much as it had helped me.

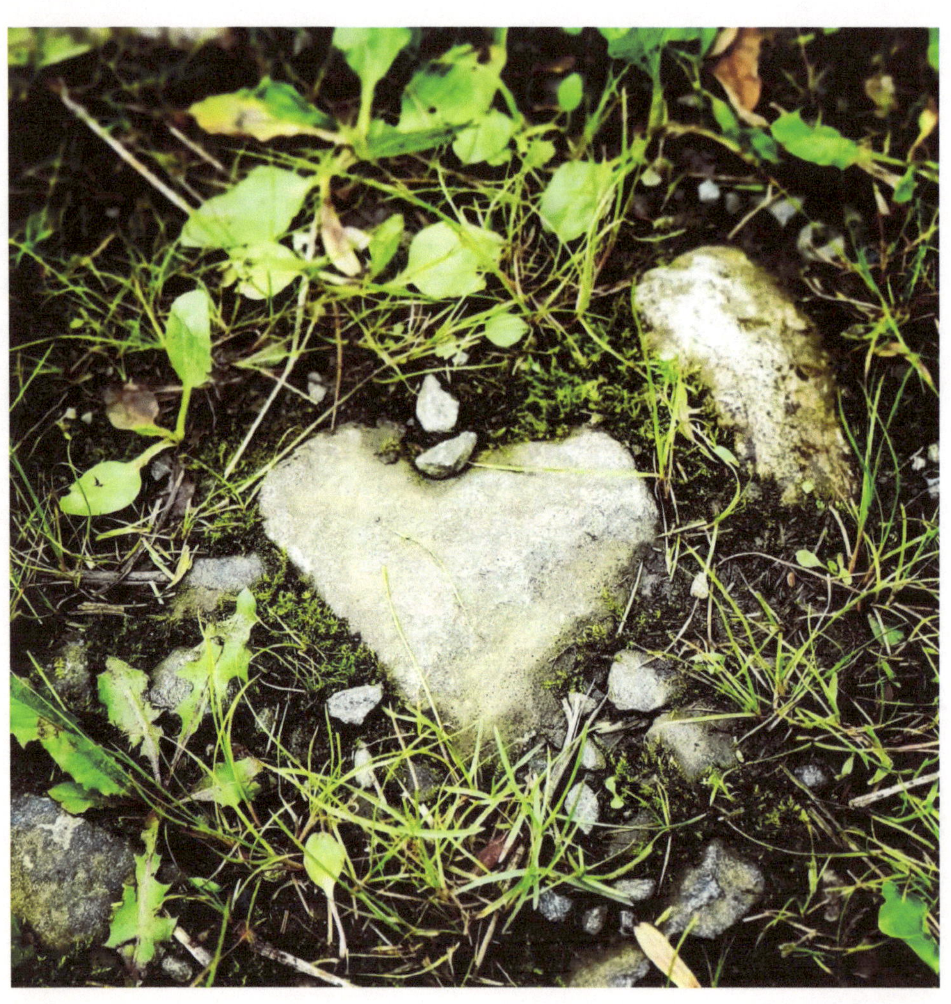

As I preserved and shared these hearts, I received beautiful stories of faith, love, strength, hopes, challenges, and fears. One common element appeared: gratitude.

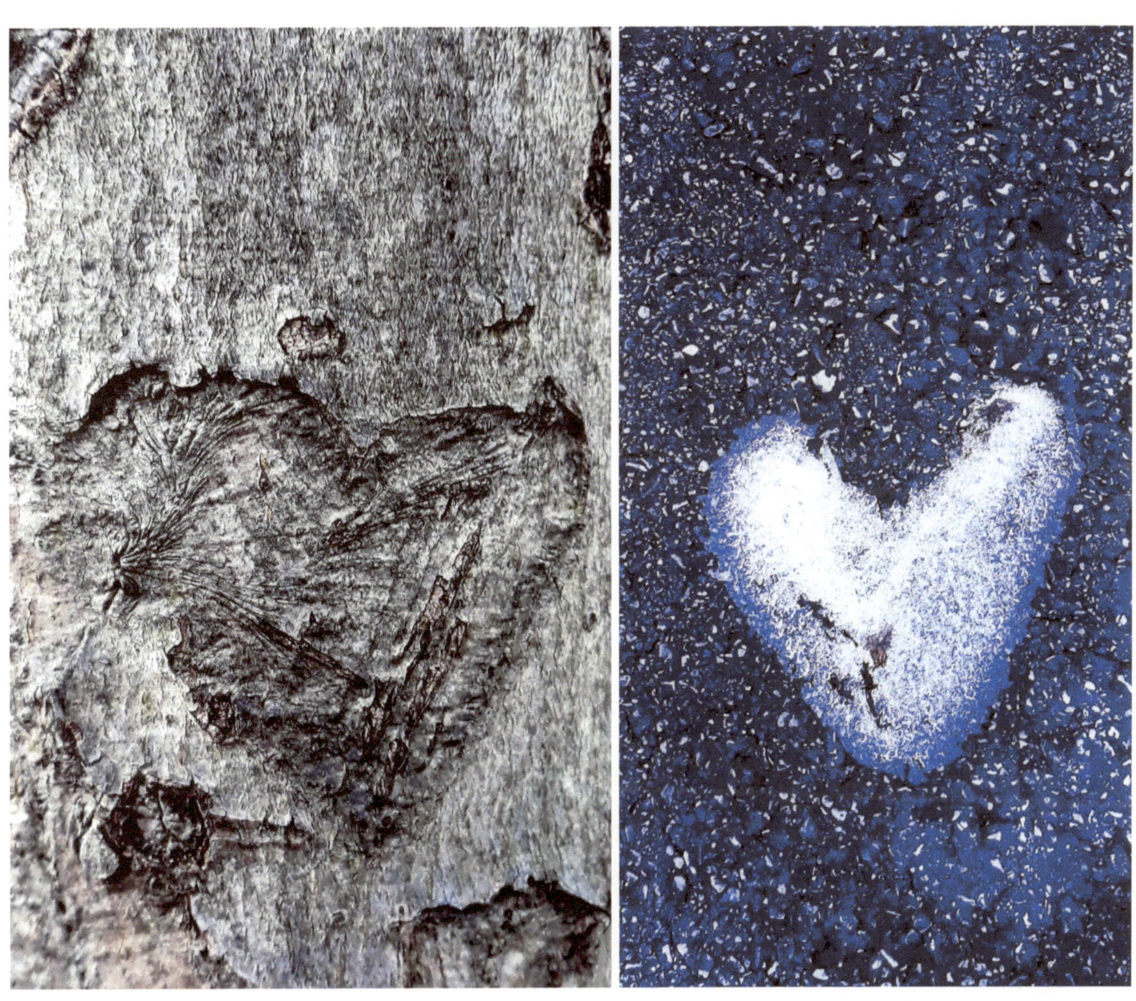

I realized we are never alone but surrounded by hints reminding us we are in this together. Love and compassion will get us through anything. And love is all around!

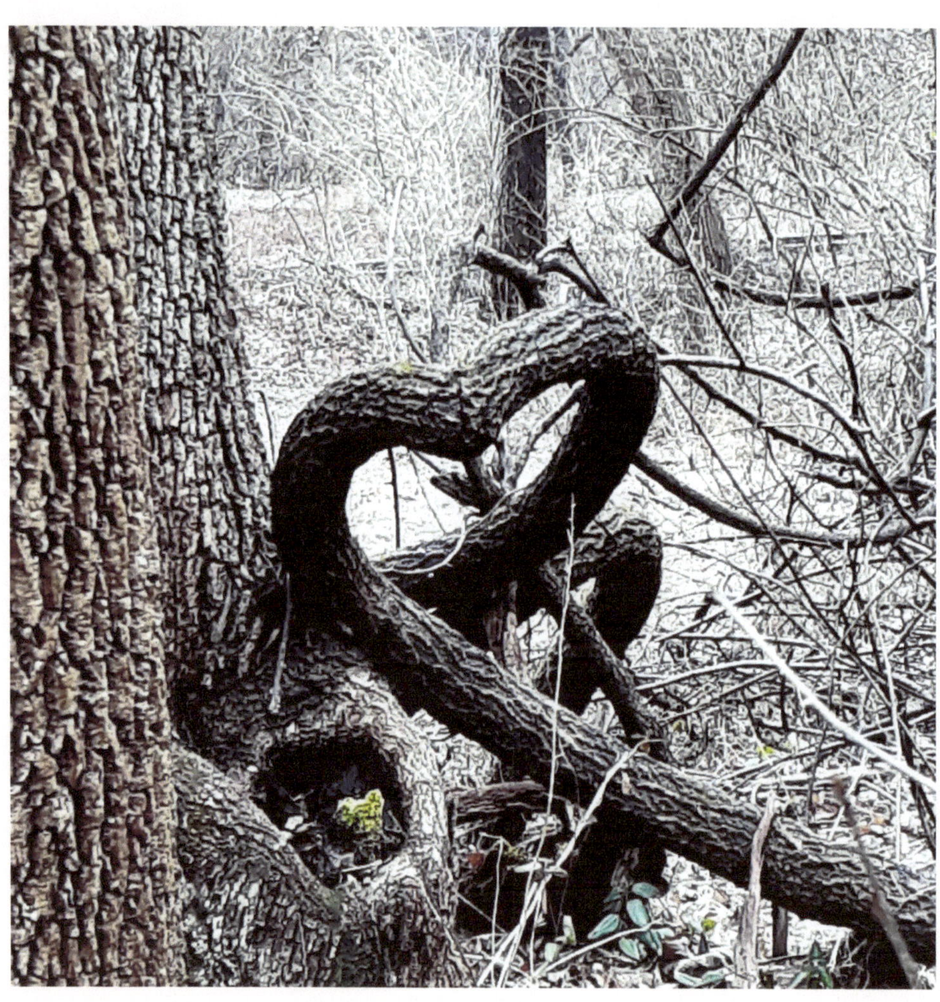

We never know where or when little hints will appear.

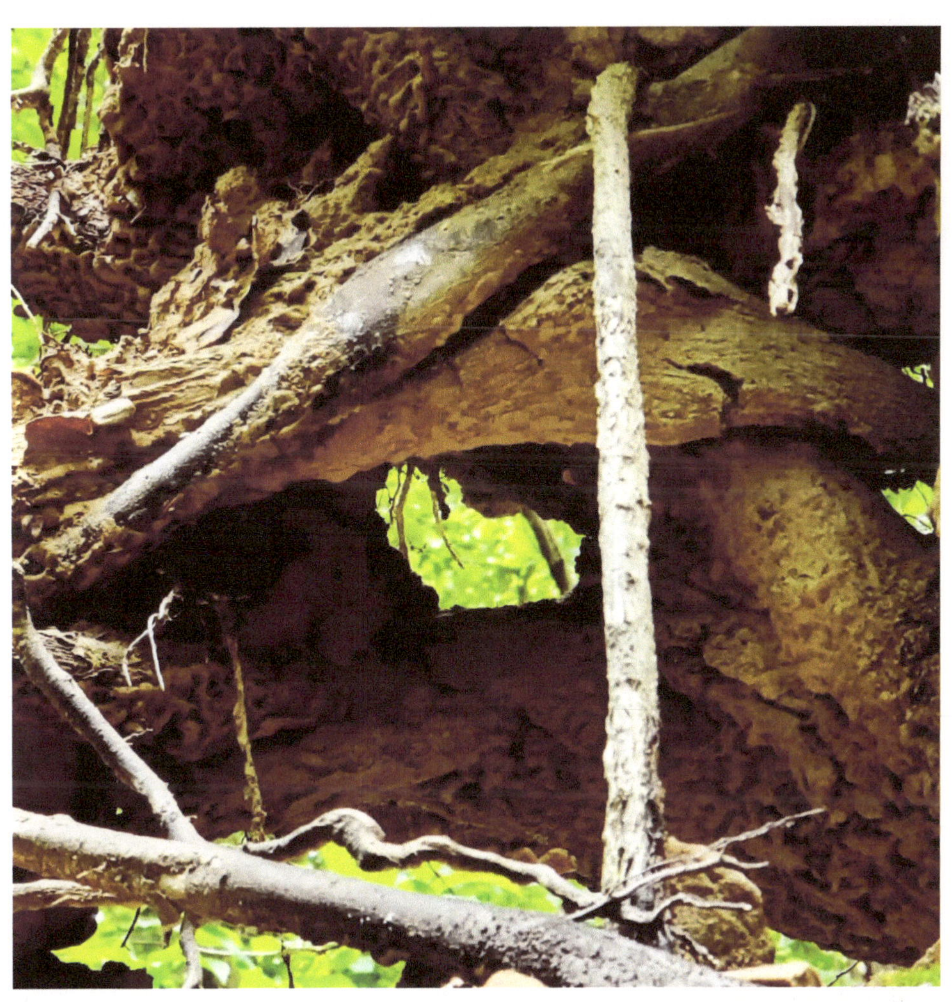

Each heart has its own story to tell, just as we do.

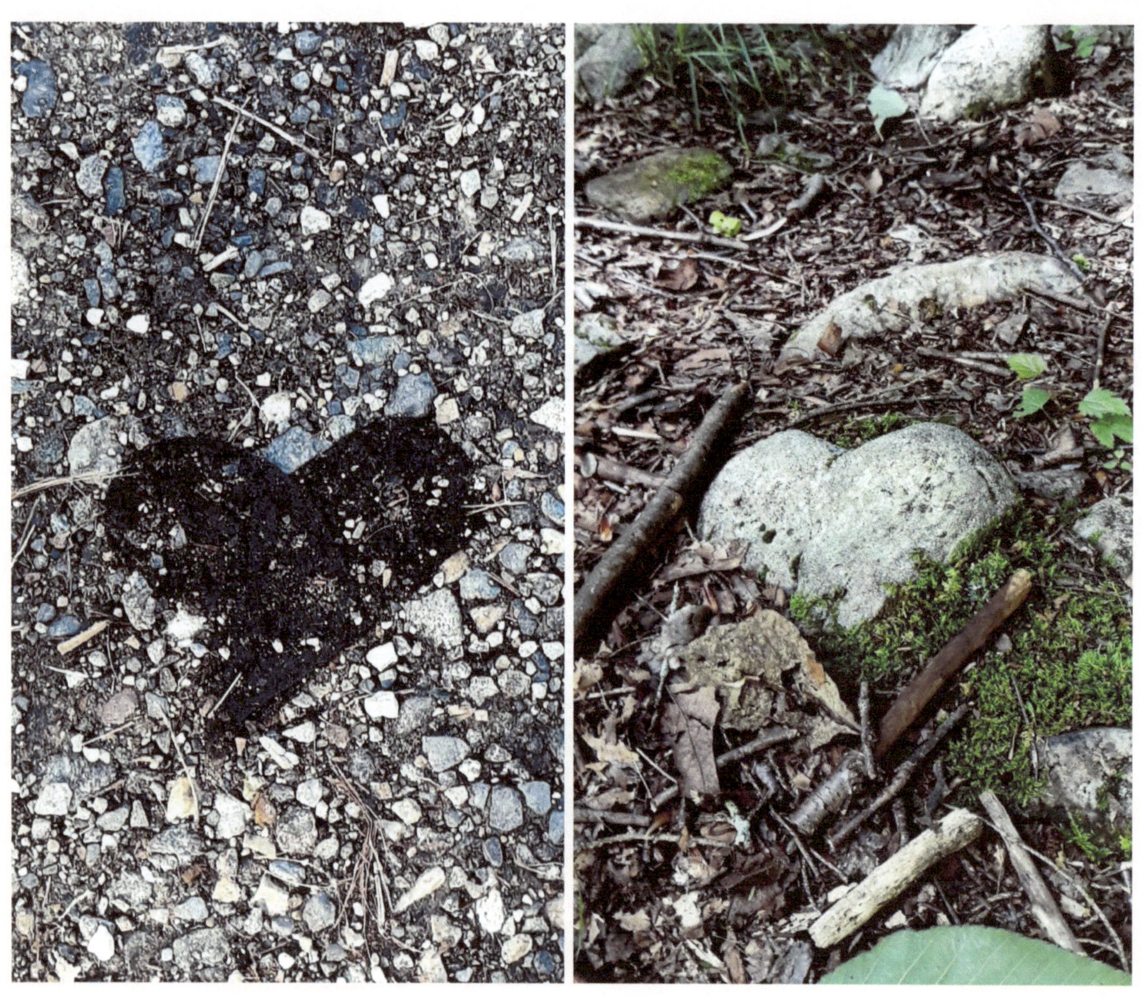

I remember finding this heart, rough around the edges and damaged. How many times had my heart felt like that? Injured hearts need additional care to love again.

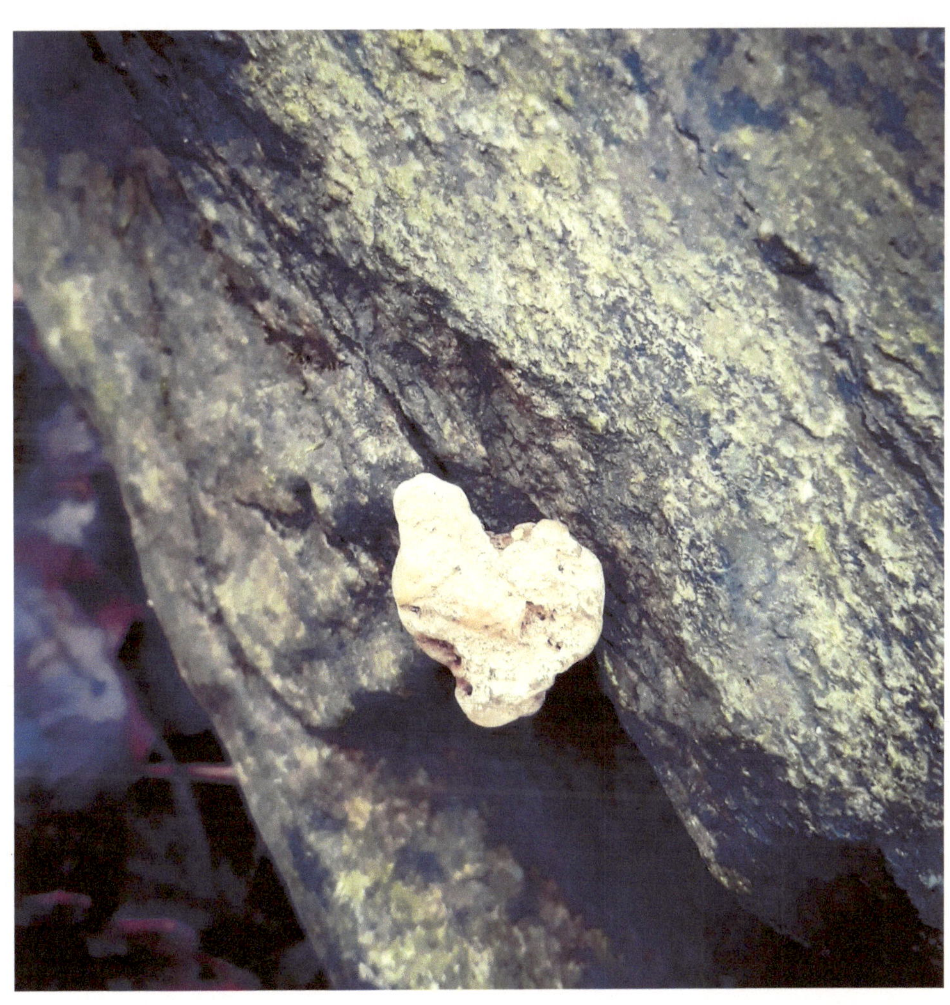

One might think this heart is broken. I see it is a warm heart breaking away from a cold stone.

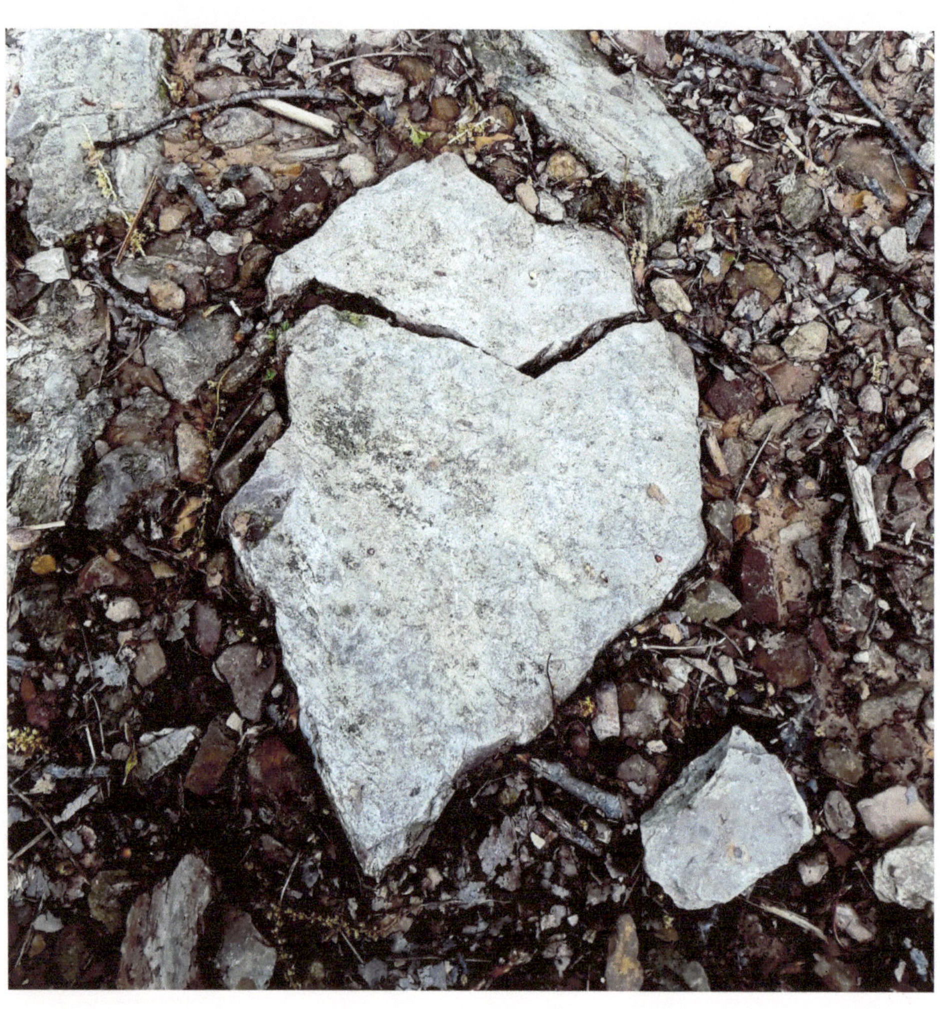

As you go about your own journey, you will come upon hearts of all sizes, shapes, and colors.

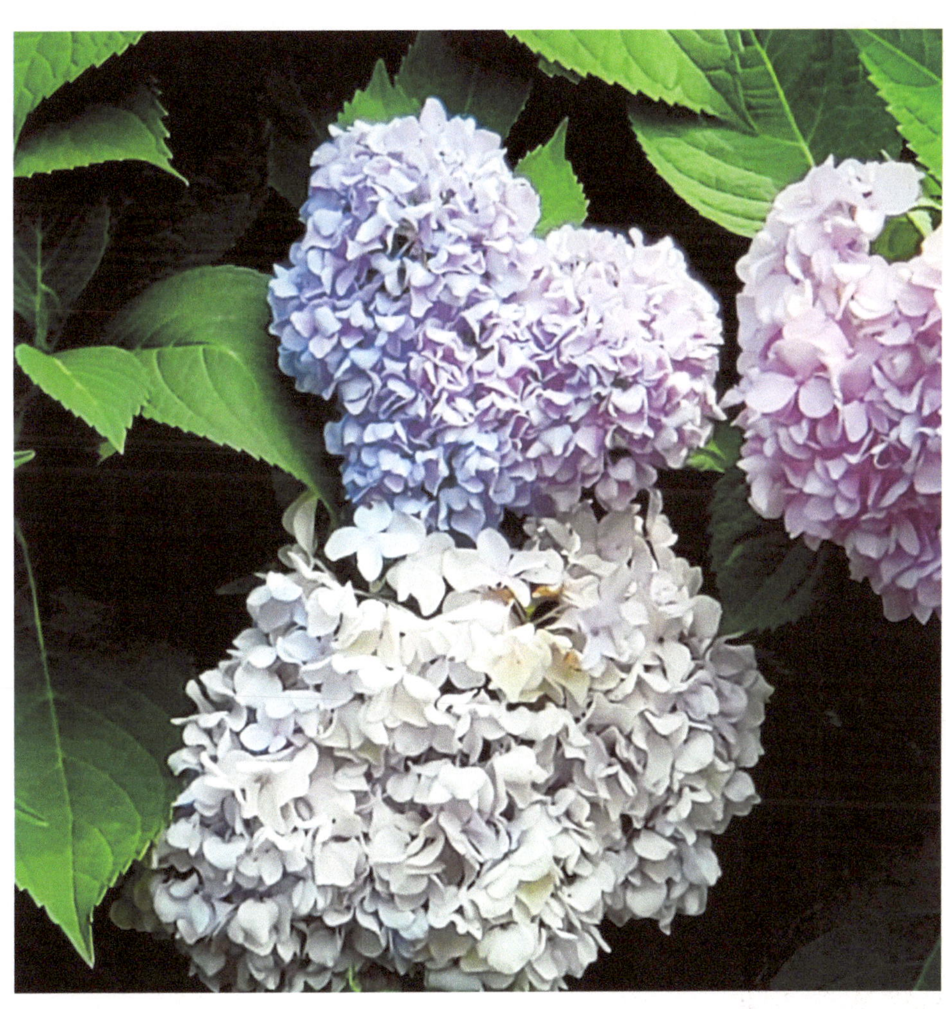

You will find them in all forms and places, like the sun and the clouds.

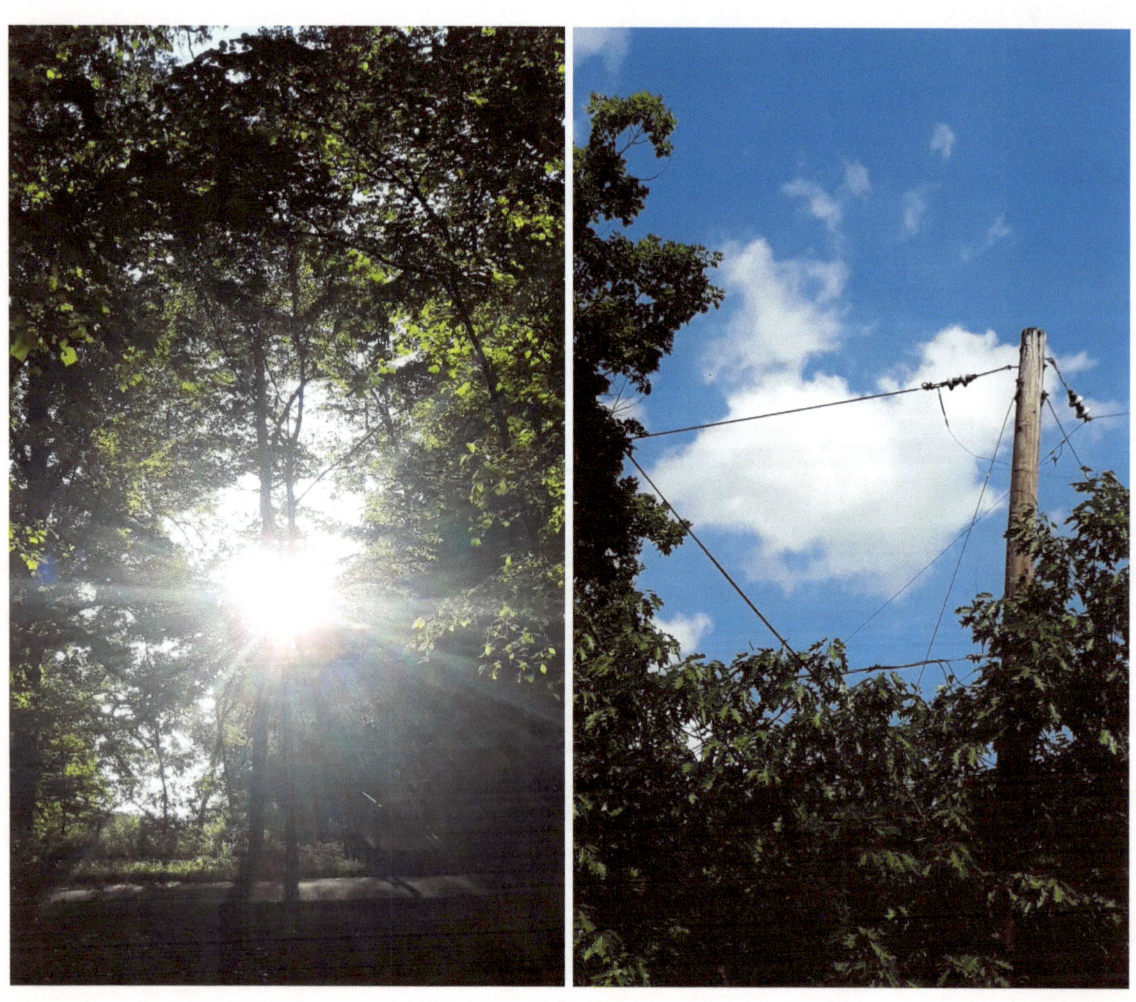

Some will appear in seeds, rocks, or leaves.

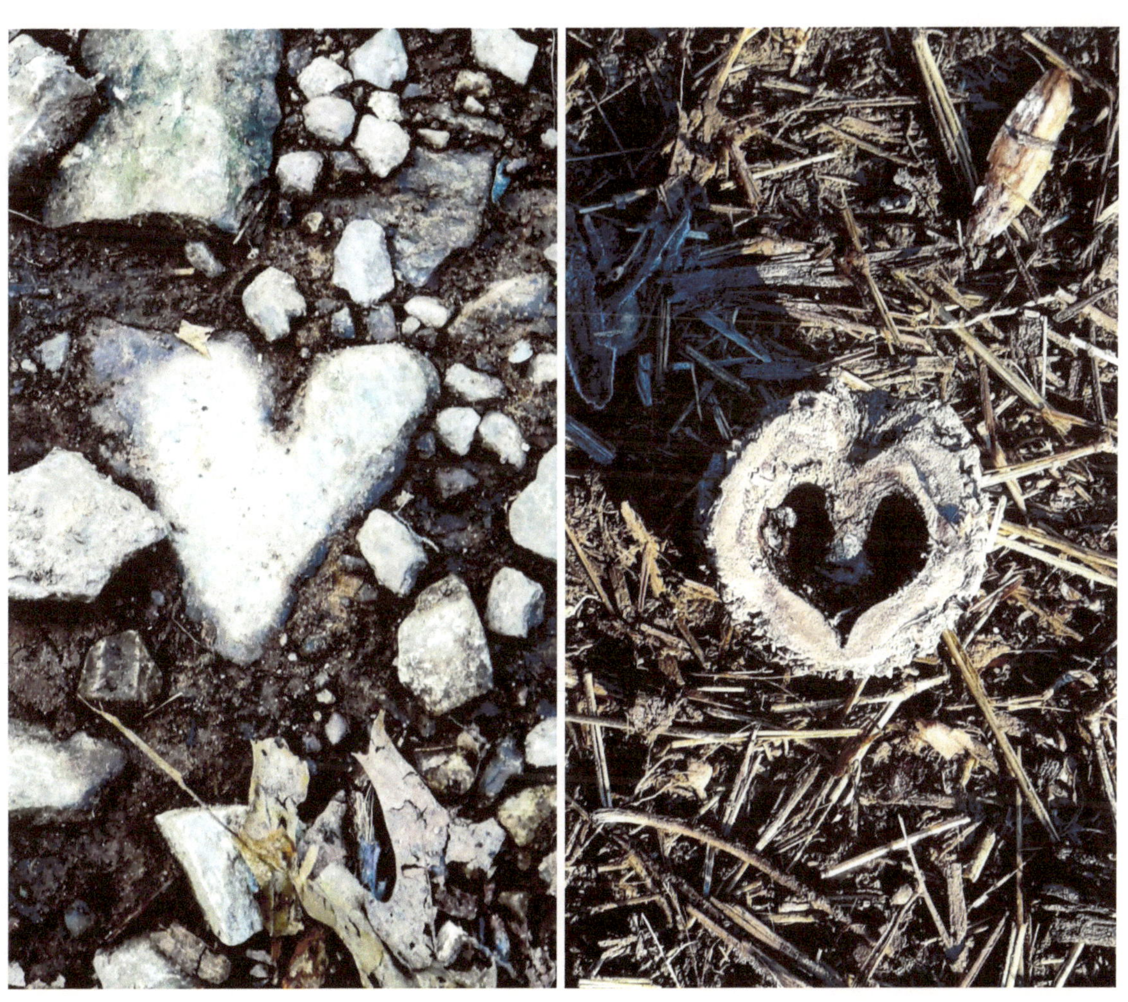

Those found in water are particularly calming and soothing.

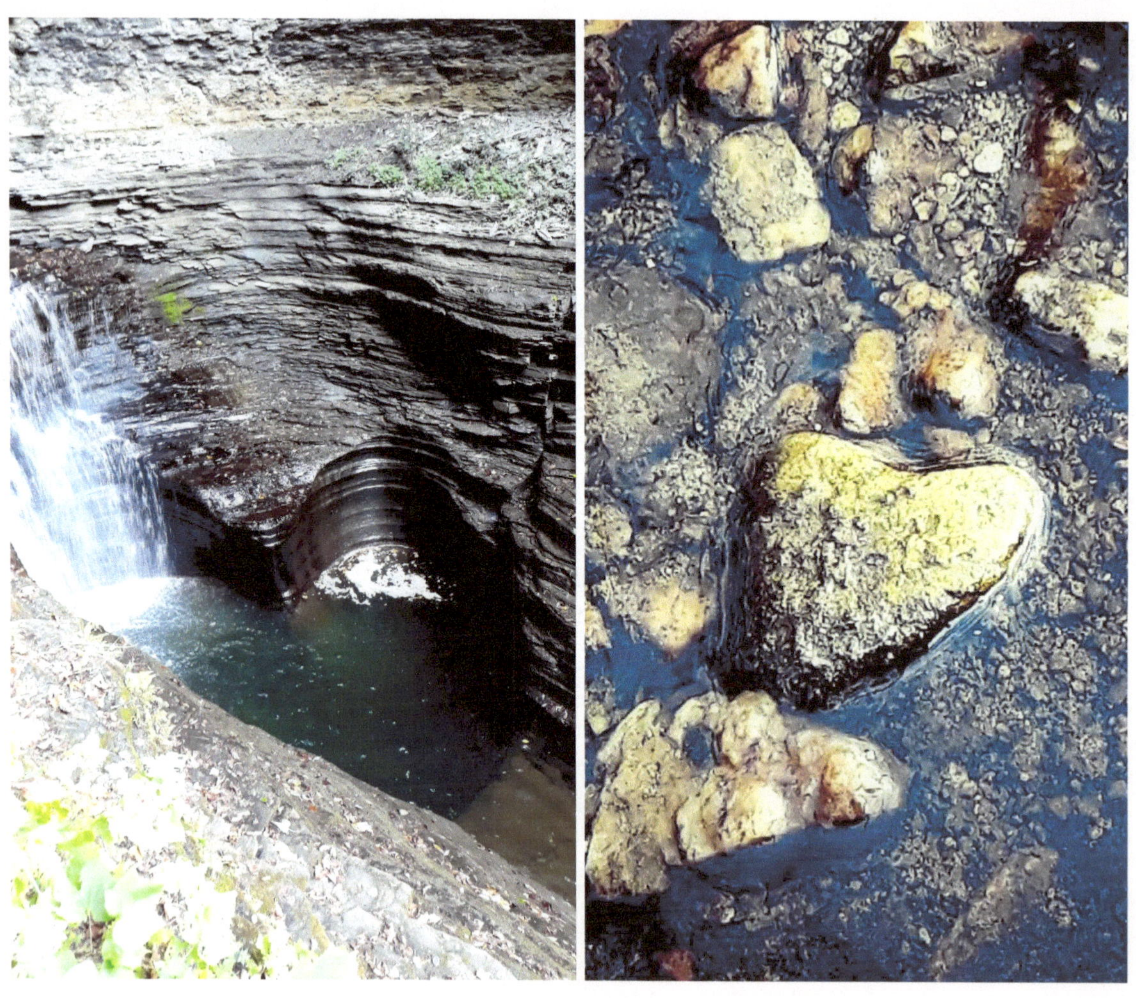

Some hearts are obvious, but others are hard to see, even though they are right in front of you.

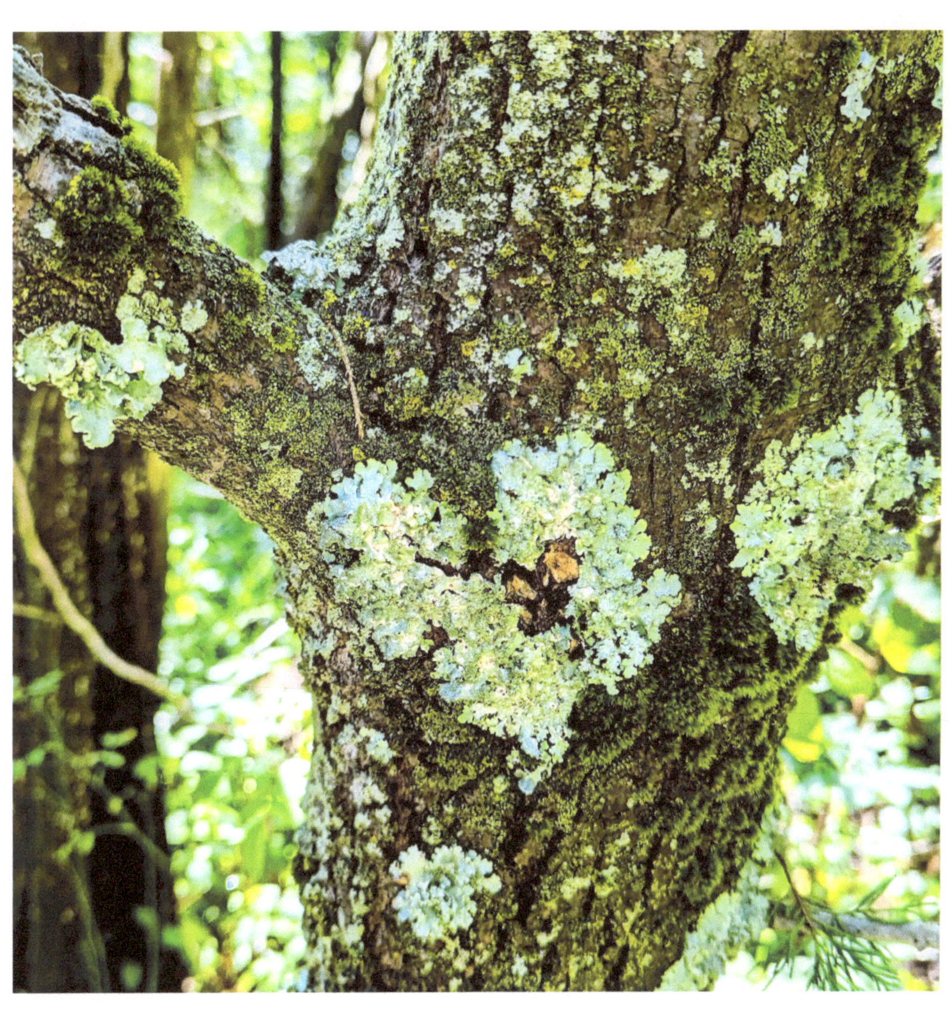

At times, someone may be trying to share their own heart. Will you see it?

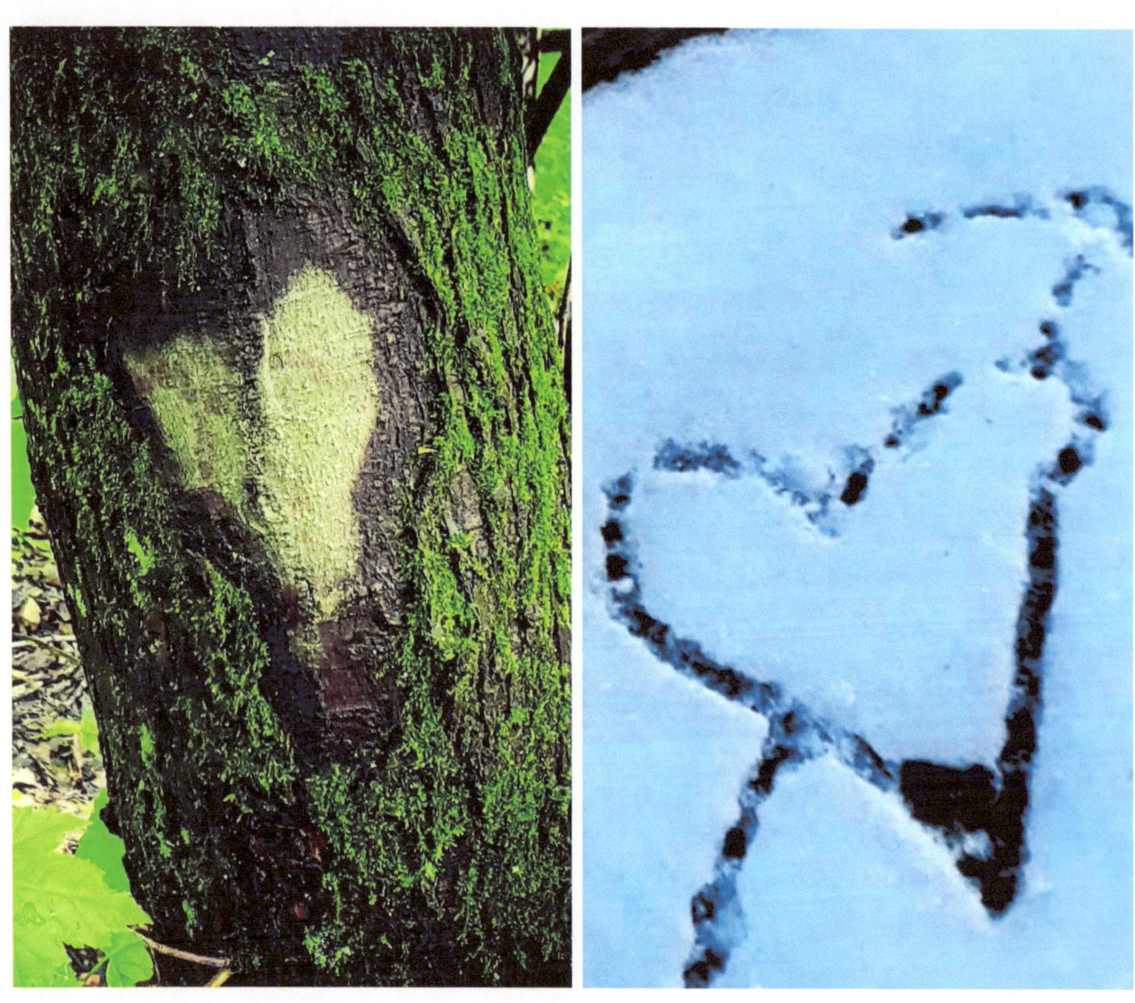

You can catch it in a fleeting moment, so be ready, be open, be joyful.

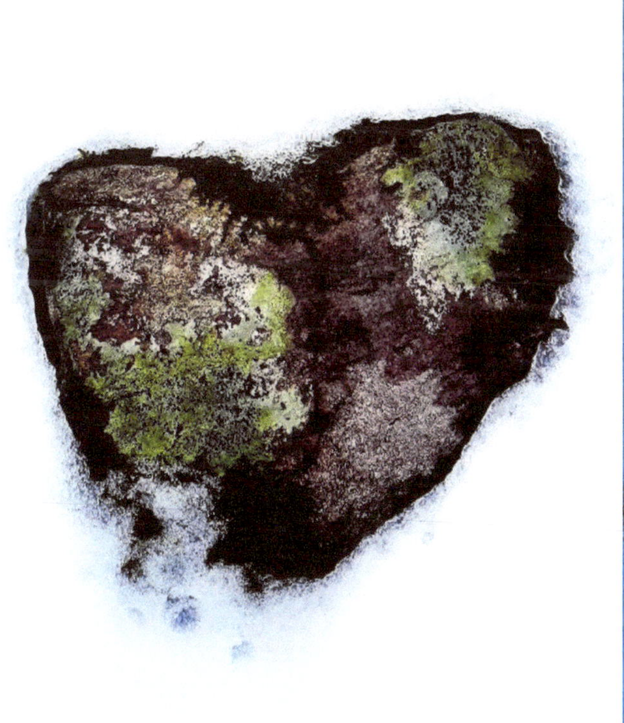

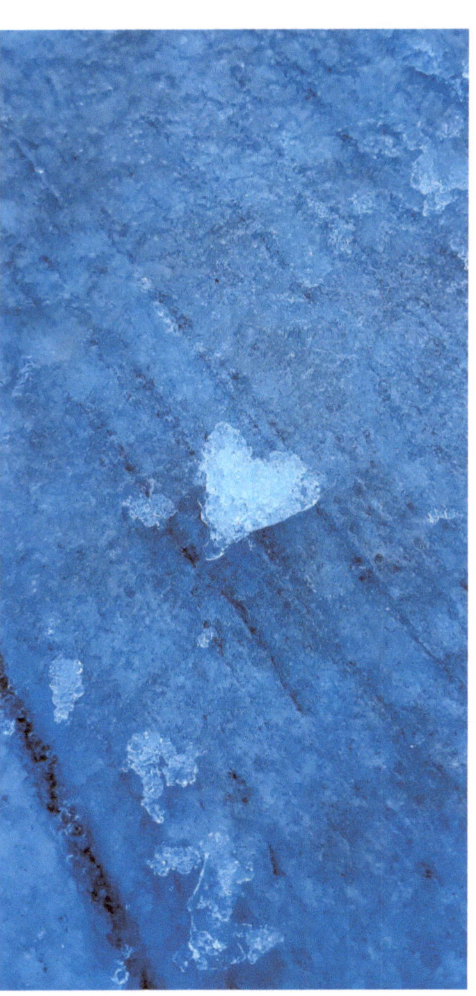

If you are having a tough day, take a moment to look outside, you never know what you might find.

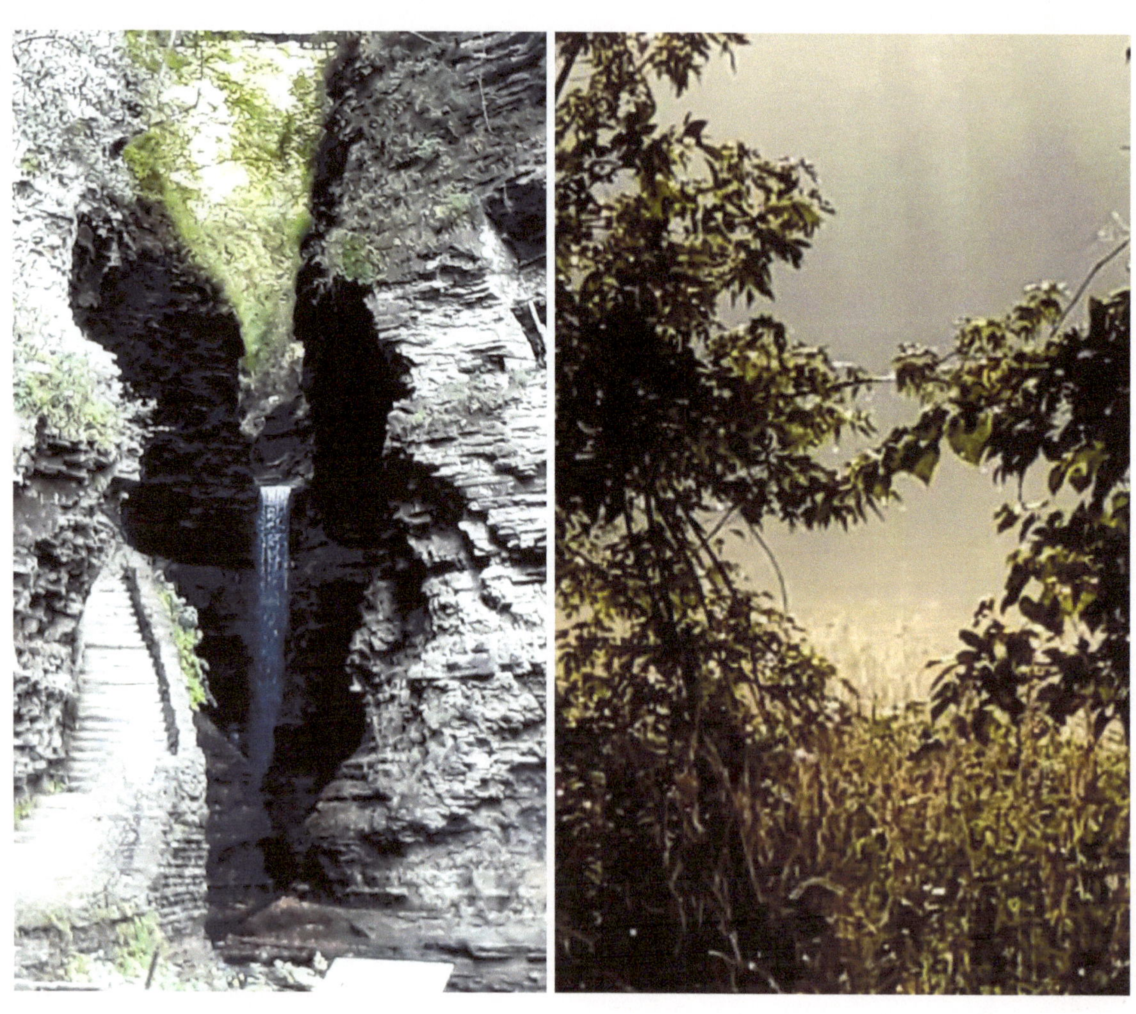

As we go through life, may you have an open and sharing heart. From one sharing heart to another.

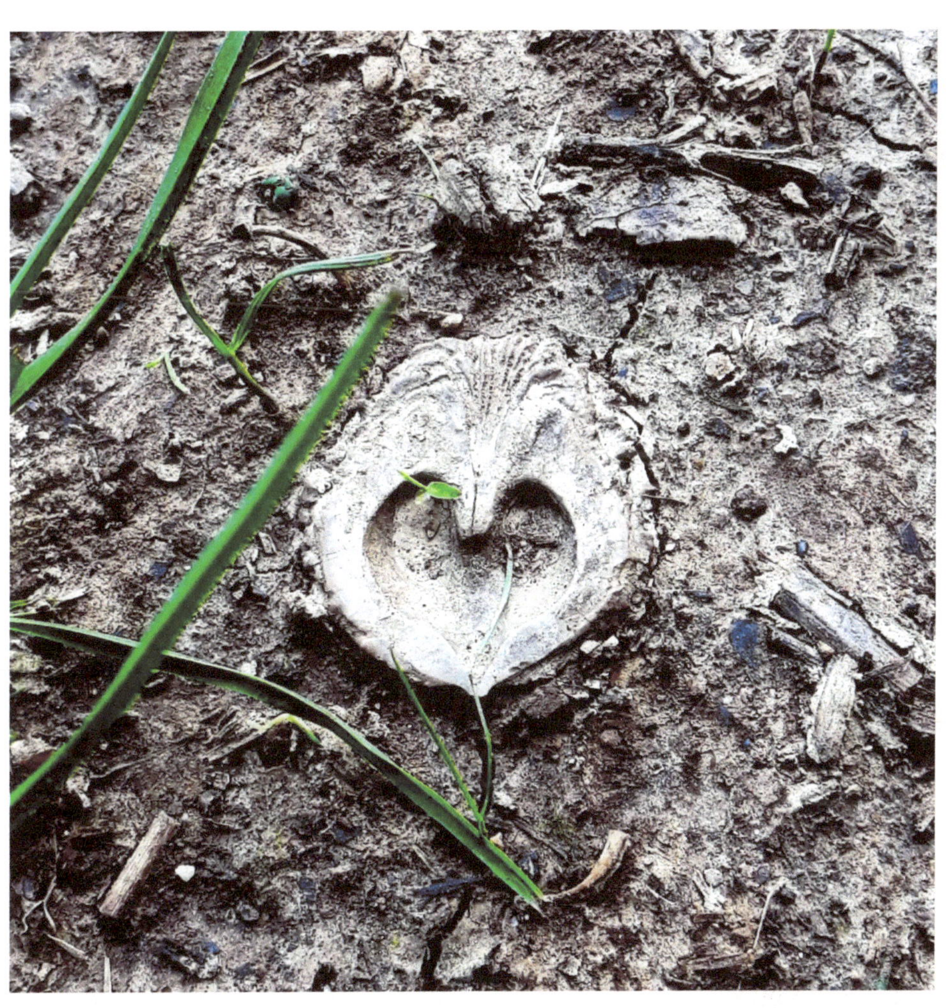

Where will your heart lead you today?

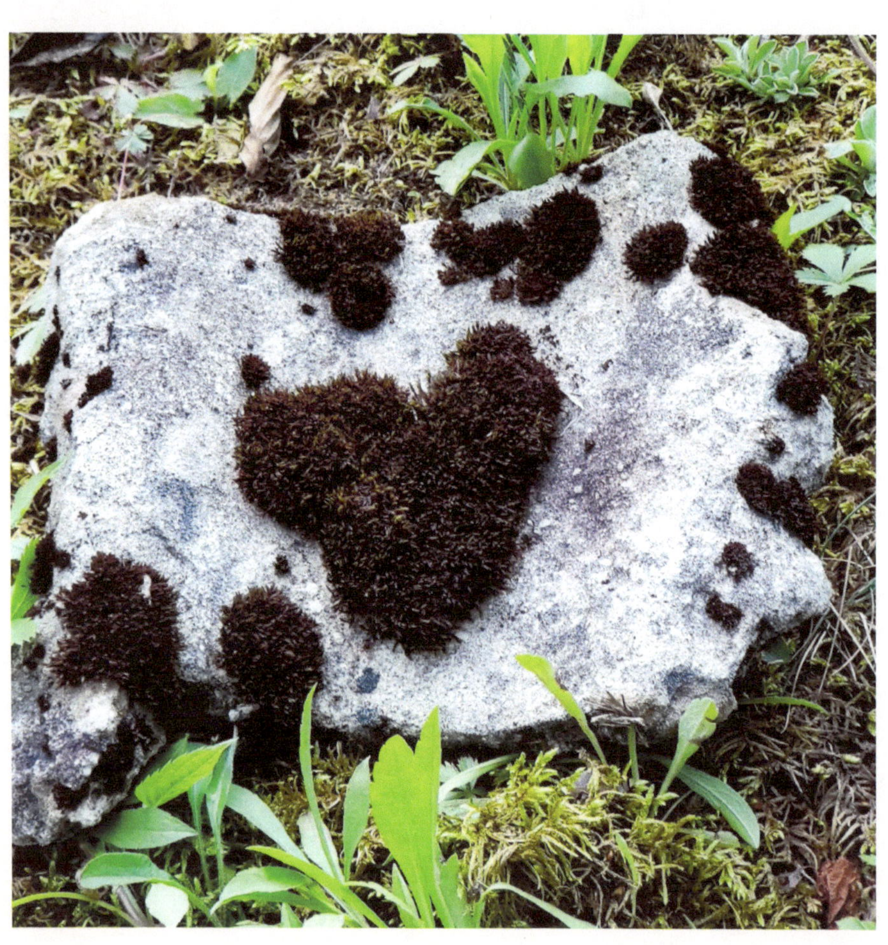

ABOUT THE AUTHOR

Karen DelRaso is an avid traveler who combines her love of adventure with her passion for volunteering and the outdoors. She spent more than two years working at a youth center in Zambia, climbed Mt. Rainer for a breast cancer fundraiser, and is involved with many local organizations, including PHW Coatesville, McKaig's Nature Education Center, African Education Program, and Total Outdoors. Karen enjoys hiking, horseback riding, rowing, and exploring new locations with family and friends. Learn more at www.lorettashearts.com.

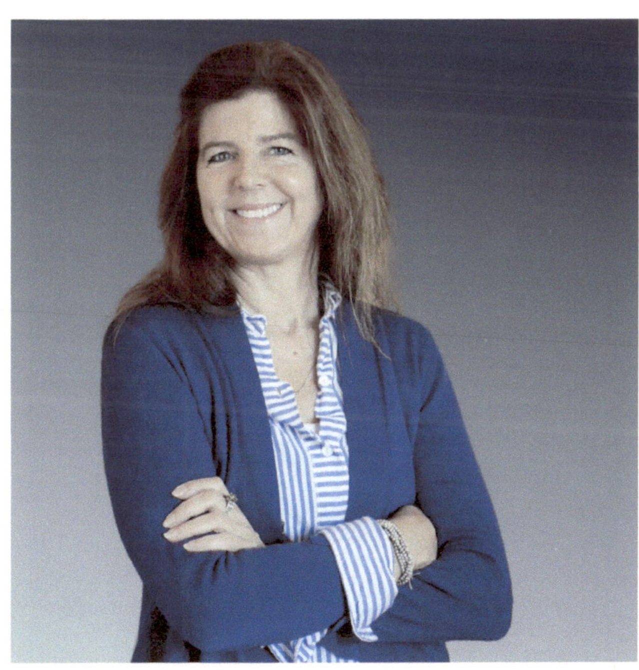

www.ingramcontent.com/pod-product-compliance
Lightning Source LLC
LaVergne TN
LVHW070207110826
845147LV00002B/523
9781950484720